CAN YOU SURVIVE

DANGEROUS DESERT ENCOUNTERS?

An Interactive
Wilderness Adventure

by Matt Doeden

CAPSTONE PRESS
a capstone imprint

Published by Capstone Press, an imprint of Capstone
1710 Roe Crest Drive, North Mankato, Minnesota 56003
capstonepub.com

Library of Congress Cataloging-in-Publication Data is available on the Library of
Congress website.
ISBN: 9781666337921 (hardcover)
ISBN: 9781666337938 (paperback)
ISBN: 9781666337945 (ebook PDF)

Summary: Could you survive being lost in the desert? Imagine being attacked by a
rattlesnake in North America's Sonoran Desert, wild dogs in Africa's Kalahari Desert, or
a redback spider in the Australian Outback. How far would you be willing to go to save
your own life? Would it work? Flip through these pages to find out!

Editorial Credits
Editor: Mandy Robbins; Designer: Heidi Thompson; Media Researchers: Jo Miller and
Pam Mitsakos; Production Specialist: Tori Abraham

Image Credits
Getty Images: CampPhoto, 27, cinoby, 103, 112, CraigRJD, 87, Westend61, 73;
Shutterstock: Agnieszka Bacal, 16, Brent Coulter, 23, Charles T. Peden, 37, CrackerClips
Stock Media, Cover, Erwin Niemand, 52, JeniFoto, 9, Johan Swanepoel, 62, Ken
Griffiths, 93, Kristian Bell, 88, Michael Potter11, 55, Ryan M. Bolton, 25, Stephanie
Buechel, 81, Try_my_best, design element, throughout, Victoria Hillman, 64,
worldswildlifewonders, 84

Printed and bound in the USA. PO4882

TABLE OF CONTENTS

LOST IN THE DESERT!

YOU find yourself stranded in the middle of the desert. Threats lurk everywhere. You're hot. You're thirsty. And most terrifying of all, deadly wildlife could creep out at every turn. Scorpions, spiders, snakes, and more. You never know what you might find—or what might find you.

What will you do when you come face-to-face with a deadly desert creature? Will you run? Will you hide? Do you have what it takes to survive? YOU CHOOSE which paths to take. Your choices will guide the story. Will you live or die? Turn the page to find out.

• Turn the page to begin your adventure.

CHAPTER 1

TRACKS IN THE SAND

The sun beats down on the dry, barren land. A wind gusts, kicking up a swirl of dust. Everywhere you look, the desert stretches out to the horizon. Dry brush clings to life in the arid conditions. Animals scurry into the shade and burrow into the ground to escape the heat. It's a constant battle for limited resources. All around you, plants and animals are doing everything they can to survive. And now you have to do the same.

• Turn the page.

"Have I been here already?" you mutter to yourself. "Am I walking in circles?" This was supposed to be an exciting adventure, but everything has gone wrong. Your precious water supply is running low. You only have a couple of bottles, and that doesn't go far in this heat.

The heat of the day drains you of your energy. But you keep moving. And the nighttime chill is a shock to the senses. Night in the desert is even more terrifying than daytime. This place may seem barren. But it's actually filled with life—and a lot of it could kill you. You need to make your way back to civilization before it's too late.

You put yourself in this situation, but you didn't realize the dangers you would face. You'll have to keep a level head to get back to safety.

You'll have to adapt and react, one step at a time. You know one thing for sure—you'll do everything you can to survive.

- To try to make it out of North America's Sonoran Desert, turn to page 11.
- To see if you can survive being lost in Africa's Kalahari Desert, turn to page 49.
- To overcome the dangers of Australia's Outback, turn to page 77.

CHAPTER 2

SURVIVING THE SONORAN DESERT

"Look up ahead," Omar says, pointing toward a few jagged boulders in the distance. They stand out against the blue sky on the otherwise flat land. "Those rocks might give us a little shade. Let's check it out."

You follow your brother to the boulders. Both of you crowd against the largest one to get as much of your bodies out of the sun as you can.

• Turn the page.

As you catch your breath, you think back to how you got into this mess. The two of you were just on a joyride.

You are new to the area, and you decided to take Omar's new 4x4 truck off-roading in the desert. He was doing tricks, spinning the truck around in tight circles and revving the engine loudly, while kicking up big clouds of dust and sand.

It was fun at first. But then the engine overheated, and something blew up. Honestly, you were lucky to not get hurt. But just like that, you found yourselves stranded in the middle of the remote desert.

There's no cell phone service way out here, and you didn't tell anyone where you went.

As you watched the steam pour out of the truck's ruined engine, you realized that no one would be coming to your rescue. You were on your own. So you did the only thing you could think to do. You gathered what few supplies you had in the truck and took off on foot. Luckily, that included a couple bottles of water. But that was three hours ago, and it feels like you haven't gotten anywhere.

"You said you remembered a town about 15 miles in this direction," you say. "How sure are you? I'm starting to feel like going on foot was a mistake."

Omar shakes his head. Sweat is pouring down his face, which is flushed from the heat. "No. It was this way. I'm almost sure of it."

• Turn the page.

"Almost?" you repeat. "We're staking our lives on almost?"

"It's this way. Besides, what other options did we have?"

You shake your head and close your eyes. Omar's probably right. But at the moment, you're exhausted and afraid. Your patience is growing thin.

Suddenly, you hear a strange sound. It's like a vibration . . . a rattle. It's coming from the bottom of the rock right behind you. It takes you a moment to process the sound. But as soon as you do, panic sets in.

"Rattlesnake!" you both shout. As you scramble to your feet, you drop your water bottle.

You look back to see it lying on the ground, right in front of a large—and aggressive-looking—western diamondback rattlesnake. You recognize the species from its signature rattle and the diamond-shaped pattern on its back. You know that rattlesnakes rarely attack humans . . . unless they feel threatened. And this snake clearly looks like it feels threatened.

"Let's go!" Omar shouts. He's always been terrified of snakes, and he's ready to run.

"Wait," you say softly. You point to the water bottle. "We can't leave that."

"So grab it," Omar says. "Just do it quick, before the snake can react."

• Turn the page.

You're not sure anyone is that quick. But the alternative is waiting for the snake to leave. And out here, in the desert sun, every minute matters. How long will that take?

- To grab the bottle and run, go to page 17.
- To convince Omar to wait for the snake to leave, turn to page 20.

"Make a distraction," you tell Omar. "Get the snake looking the other direction."

Omar steps to one side of the rock. He waves his arms and shouts at the snake, while you stand perfectly still. The snake turns its head toward Omar, rattling its tail in warning.

This is your chance. Moving as quietly and as quickly as you can, you dart forward and reach out for the bottle.

The snake senses the movement. In a flash, it strikes. You yelp in pain, as its long, sharp fangs sink into the flesh of your forearm. Omar screams!

You stumble back and fall to the ground as the snake slithers away into a crack in the rock.

• Turn the page.

Omar rushes to your side. The snake injected venom deep in your arm. It's already pumping through your bloodstream. You can feel the symptoms—you're light-headed. Your vision is a little blurry. It's only going to get worse until you get medical help. "We have to move," you say. "I've read about rattlesnake bites. It's only a matter of time before this makes me really sick . . . or worse. I need to get to a hospital."

Omar helps you to your feet. The two of you head out into the desert, desperately looking for signs of civilization. Already, the effects of the bite are slowing you down, but you try to ignore the discomfort and focus on finding help.

After about 20 minutes, you come across a dirt road. It's really just a few ruts in the ground, but it's something. "Maybe this leads back to that town," you say. You start stumbling down the road. But after a few more minutes of walking, a wave of dizziness hits and you double over, vomiting.

"You need to rest," Omar says. "It's almost evening. The sun isn't so strong now. Wait here and rest. I'll go ahead for help. I can move a lot faster without you."

Omar might be right. But somehow, waiting here alone feels like a death sentence.

- To send Omar ahead to find help, turn to page 26.
- To continue down the road, turn to page 31.

You shake your head. Waiting in the hot sun isn't great, but trying to move quicker than a snake is about the worst idea you can imagine.

"We need that water," you tell Omar, "But there's no way we can move faster than a snake. We don't have any choice but to try to wait it out. It doesn't want a confrontation any more than we do. It will leave eventually."

Luckily, it doesn't take long. You and Omar back away, and the snake soon slithers under the rock. With the precious water bottle back in your hand, you continue on your way.

Hours pass. You take small sips from your water bottles to stay hydrated. But it's exhausting. Finally, as the sun dips in the sky, the temperature begins to drop.

"We're going to need to find a place to wait out the night," Omar says.

"What about up there?" you suggest, pointing to a tall, rocky ridge in the distance.

Omar is exhausted, and the thought of more hiking makes him groan. He finds a large, flat rock nearby. A few spiny saguaro cactuses grow along its edge. "My legs are aching. What about just waiting it out over there?"

You look back and forth. Omar has a point. Every bit of energy you spend out here matters. But it might be worth it to get to higher ground. You never know what you might see from up there. And if any desert predators are out hunting, you may have a chance of seeing them before they see you.

• To hike to the ridge, turn to page 22.
• To stay here on the rock, turn to page 24.

"The sun is setting fast," you say. "I think that ridge is our best bet. It will get us to high ground, where we can get a better view of our surroundings. I know you're tired, Omar. I am too. But I think it's worth pressing on."

Omar grumbles a bit, but he doesn't argue with your decision. So once again, you set out. You're both exhausted, but you take it one step at a time. By the time the two of you scramble to the top of the ridge, the sun is down. Night is falling over the desert, and the temperature is dropping fast.

That's when you see the light. It's a yellow glow in the west. "The town!" you shout. It's hard to tell how far away it is, but you know it's within reach.

"Let's go!" Omar says. "Come on, what are we waiting for?"

"It's going to be pitch black out here," you argue. "Do we want to do this in the dark? Would it be safer to wait here until sunrise?"

- To head out into the night, turn to page 28.
- To try to get some sleep here, turn to page 38.

You shrug. "Okay, we can stay here," you agree. Omar plops himself down on the rock and starts rubbing his feet. You kick off your boots and take a look at your water bottle. It's less than half full. And Omar's has even less. You're going to have to get started at the break of daylight. With so little water remaining, time isn't on your side.

It's a restless night. You snooze a little off and on. But mostly, you just lie there, uncomfortable and afraid. When morning comes, you're even more tired than you were when you stopped. You grab your boots and start to pull them on.

"OW!" you shout, feeling a sharp pain in your foot. You jerk your foot out of the boot, and a huge spider comes tumbling out as well. It's a big, brown, hairy tarantula! The spider scrambles away as you grab your foot, rubbing the spot where you feel a sharp, throbbing pain.

"That thing bit me!" you tell Omar, rubbing your foot. Spiders have always creeped you out. You're not sure how dangerous a tarantula bite is. You're pretty sure it's not going to kill you, but the idea of the huge spider's venom in your blood makes your skin crawl. You feel a powerful urge to clean out the wound. But then you'd have even less water left.

- To shake out your boots and put them on, turn to page 30.
- To use a little of your water to clean the bite wound, turn to page 40.

You don't want to wait here alone. But Omar is right. You're slowing him down. Resting here might be your best chance at survival. Omar gives you a hug and leaves one of the water bottles with you. Then he begins jogging down the dirt road. You lie down and try to slow your heartbeat. Your only job now is to stay alive.

The sun slowly dips lower in the sky. The temperature drops. Your chest feels heavy, and you have to work hard just to breathe.

As night falls, your body shakes with chills. You take small sips of water to fight off dehydration. "Just hold on," you tell yourself.

The howl of a coyote echoes across the night. A few minutes later, you hear it again . . . only closer this time. Much closer.

A half-moon shines just a little light on the desert landscape. It's enough to see the shadow. The coyote is close. Too close. And you're in no condition to defend yourself.

• To lie quietly and hope the coyote doesn't notice you, turn to page 33.

• To shout at the coyote, turn to page 35.

27

You didn't like the idea of striking blindly out into the night. But now you have somewhere to go. And suddenly Omar isn't complaining about more hiking.

It's slow going in the dark. Omar's phone still has a little charge, so you use it as a flashlight. But after about an hour, it blinks off. "Battery's dead," he sighs as he tucks the useless phone into his pocket.

You can still see the glow of the town's lights in the distance. You can hardly wait to get there—and the occasional howl of a coyote in the distance only makes you want to go faster. But now, in total darkness, you find yourself stumbling over every rock. What seemed close now seems a very long way away.

At one point, Omar falls face-first onto the rocky desert floor. He gets up with a few nasty scrapes on his knees and a cut on his forehead. You know that every step could lead to a twisted ankle—or worse. Is it worth the risk to keep going?

You look around for a place you could stop and rest. But in the dark, everything looks the same. Here is as good as anywhere.

- To rest here until morning, turn to page 38.
- To try to make your way in the dark, turn to page 44.

You know tarantula bites are almost never serious. It feels a little like a bee's sting. So, as much as you want to clean your foot, you resist the urge to use any of your precious water. Instead, you check your boots for any other critters that may have made a home inside. Finding no other threats, you lace them up and prepare to head out.

"You ready?" you ask Omar. He nods.

There's no time to waste. You need to find help, and you need to find it quickly.

Turn to page 42.

You shake your head. "There's no way I'm staying here, alone in the desert overnight. Let's keep moving."

It's slow going. Walking makes your heart pump hard, speeding up the venom's progress through your body. Your arm is swollen and painful. Your vision gets blurrier by the minute. You're sweating like crazy.

About 10 minutes later, you begin to feel cold. You notice that you're not sweating anymore. Omar is saying something to you, but everything sounds very far away. In the back of your mind, you realize that all your sweating has left you badly dehydrated. The lack of water combined with the damage that the venom is doing is a one-two punch. Your body can't handle it.

• Turn the page.

You collapse. The world goes black. Your brother does all he can to save you. But it isn't enough. Your time is up.

THE END

To follow another path, turn to page 9.
To learn more about life in the desert, turn to page 99.

You doubt you have the strength to do anything but lay still. Your heart is racing. Fear wells up inside you until you feel like throwing up. But you remain perfectly still. Totally quiet. Maybe . . . just maybe . . . if you're completely silent, the threat will finally go away.

A minute passes. Two.

Then you hear it. Small footsteps—the scraping of claws on rock. Were they coming toward you or going away? You close your eyes and strain to hear every tiny sound.

You try to calm yourself, but panic is setting in. You feel a hot breath across your face. It smells like rancid meat.

• Turn the page.

Coyote attacks on humans are rare, but they are opportunists. In the harsh desert, they must take advantage of any easy meal they can find. And tonight, that's you. You're too weak to fight or run. You might have survived the snakebite. But there's no chance that you'll make it through this.

THE END

To follow another path, turn to page 9.
To learn more about life in the desert, turn to page 99.

You're exhausted and defenseless. If the coyote comes for you, there won't be a thing you can do to stop it. So you do the only thing you can. You summon all of your strength and let out a roar. You make it as loud and as deep as you can. You shout until you can't shout anymore. And then, every few minutes, you do it again.

It's the only strategy you have, and it works. The next time you hear that howl, it's from a long way away. The coyote is off in search of less threatening prey.

You doze off and on throughout the night. By sunrise, you're in rough shape. Your water is gone. Your arm is swollen and painful to the touch. You can't feel your feet. You begin to come to terms with the idea that you're going to die out here, alone. You imagine Omar returning only to find your lifeless body.

• Turn the page.

That's when you hear it. A low thumping sound in the sky. You squint and look up. Everything is blurry, but you can make out the shape. It's a medical helicopter! Omar did it!

The helicopter lands in a fury of dust. As the EMTs load you into the cab, you breathe a sigh of relief. "Your brother is waiting for you at the hospital," says a young dark-haired woman. "He ran almost 10 miles in the middle of the night to get help. He's in the hospital now, recovering from dehydration." She gives you a dose of antivenin to fight off the venom. "You'll be recovering for a while too, but you're going to be okay."

It was a close call. But you survived your terrifying ordeal in the desert.

THE END

To follow another path, turn to page 9.
To learn more about life in the desert, turn to page 99.

Striking out into the darkness doesn't seem like a great idea. So the two of you huddle up and wait out the night. You snooze a little, but you're cold, uncomfortable, and eager to get started toward the town. Just before sunrise, when the sky is beginning to turn orange, Omar lets out a sudden yelp, holding his ankle. "OWWWW! Something bit me!"

There's just enough light in the sky to make out the culprit. A small, brown scorpion scurries away across the sandy rocks. It's a bark scorpion.

"It's not a bite, genius," you tell Omar. "It's a sting. As long as you're not allergic to it, it's not going to kill you."

The sting swells up, and Omar is miserable. But with light in the sky, you head out in the direction of town.

It takes you three hours, and all of your water is gone. But you finally get there. The two of you stumble into a convenience store. The clerk hurries out from behind the counter, bringing you food and water, while you call for help.

You made it. And you've got a story to tell your friends. But you don't think you'll go off-roading in the desert again any time soon.

THE END

To follow another path, turn to page 9.
To learn more about life in the desert, turn to page 99.

You just have to clean your wound. You grab your water bottle and splash a little of the water onto the bite, rubbing it to try to work out the venom that you know is now pumping through your veins. You try to use just a few drops, but in your hurry, you knock the bottle over. All of your water spills out. Within moments, that life-giving resource is nothing but a wet blotch on the desert floor.

It's a critical mistake. By midmorning, the sun is roasting you. Omar shares what little water he has. But it's not enough. By noon, you're too dehydrated to move anymore. You collapse in what little shade a large saguaro cactus can give you.

"We'll just have to hope someone finds us," Omar says in a dry, raspy voice. "Maybe there will be a hiker. Or a search party. Or . . . something."

You nod, trying to pretend that it's true. But in reality, both of you know that no help is coming as you fade in and out of consciousness. You gave it your best shot, but you failed to make it out of the desert alive.

THE END

To follow another path, turn to page 9.
To learn more about life in the desert, turn to page 99.

The two of you head west, with the rising sun at your back. You limp along on your swollen foot, taking small sips of water along the way.

By noon, the sun is baking you. You're getting a serious sunburn. But then you hear a familiar noise—the sound of a semitruck. "A highway!" Omar shouts.

It's about half a mile away. Despite your exhaustion, you run for it. Within minutes, another vehicle comes along. You're in luck—it's a state trooper! You wave down the patrol car. The officer pulls over and hurries out of her car.

"Looks like you two have had a rough couple of days," she says. "Is anyone injured?"

"I have a spider bite, but otherwise we're okay," you reply. "Just hungry, tired, and really thirsty."

"Climb in," she says, opening the back door of the car. "I've got a few water bottles. We have a patrol station just up the road. I'll get you there and make sure everything is all right."

You sit back, crack open a bottle of cold water, and take a long, slow drink. Nothing has ever tasted better in your life.

THE END

To follow another path, turn to page 9.
To learn more about life in the desert, turn to page 99.

The town seems so close now. All you have to do is just keep moving. For the next 20 minutes, you plod along. You trip once, falling hard onto your knees.

"It's so dark," Omar says. "What I wouldn't give for a bright full moon tonight."

Suddenly, you hear a grunt and the sound of tumbling rocks. Omar screams.

"Where are you?" you call out.

"Stop! Don't walk any farther," Omar answers with a weak voice. "There's a big drop. I fell. I'm hurt . . . bad."

On your hands and knees, you creep forward and find the edge of a large rock ledge. From the sounds of Omar's voice, he fell at least 9 feet.

"How bad are you hurt?" you call down.

Omar groans. "I don't know. I think I broke my leg. Took a pretty good hit to my head too."

You keep Omar talking all night, trying to distract him from his pain and the growing fear in his voice. You talk about home, about what you want to eat when you get there, and about anything else that comes to mind.

When morning arrives, you see the damage. Omar is in bad shape. His leg is definitely broken, and he's really scraped up. "Hold tight," you tell him. "I'll get help."

In the daylight, with a clear direction to follow, it only takes you about an hour to find help. You stagger into a small town and call 911 from a gas station.

• Turn the page.

You explain where Omar is located. "Stay where you are," the operator tells you. "We'll get your brother, and we'll send someone to check on you too. Help is on the way."

You sit down and let out an exhausted sigh. You're both going to survive the ordeal. But your brother has a long recovery in front of him. You're just lucky that you didn't fall too. You shiver when you think of how badly things would have ended if you'd both been hurt.

THE END

To follow another path, turn to page 9.
To learn more about life in the desert, turn to page 99.

CHAPTER 3

SURVIVING THE KALAHARI

It was supposed to be the sightseeing tour of a lifetime—a hike into the depths of Africa's Kalahari Desert. It's one of the most biologically diverse deserts on the planet, filled with amazing creatures from snakes and scorpions to lions, cheetahs, and rhinos. But when you and your sister wandered away from your tour group to check out some sand dunes, you lost track of time.

• Turn the page.

"The tour bus! It's leaving!" Maria shouts.

"Run!" you reply. The two of you chase off after the bus, but it's too late.

"I thought we had more time," you say, staring as the cloud of dust kicked up by the bus tires fades away into the distance. Slowly, the seriousness of the situation starts to dawn on you. You're stranded in the desert, far from help.

"What were we thinking?" Maria grumbles. "Mom and Dad are going to be worried sick when the tour bus comes back tonight and we're not on it."

You take her hand. "Let's be calm," you say. "Once they realize we're missing, they'll send help. Someone will be coming for us. We just have to stay safe until then."

What you don't say is that it might take a long time for that help to arrive. You left your hats hanging on the top of your seats in the back of the bus. The tour guide probably included them in the head count when the bus took off. Who knows when they'll realize the two of you aren't there. It was a full-day tour through the heart of the Kalahari Desert. The rest of the group might not know where you separated from them, so they won't know exactly where to look. And there are only a few hours of daylight left. You're afraid you're going to have to spend the night out here.

You look around, knowing that you might need to find a place to hunker down. Each of you wanders in a different direction, looking for a spot that seems safe and comfortable. Suddenly, Maria lets out a scream. "Ewwwwww!" she shouts. You rush to her side.

• Turn the page.

She's standing in front of a half-eaten springbok carcass. Something has torn the young gazelle to shreds. Flies buzz all around it. You prepare yourself for the terrible smell of rotting meat—but the carcass doesn't really stink yet. That means it must be a fairly recent kill.

"What could do that?" Maria asks, her voice shaking.

You shrug. "Wild dogs, leopards, lions . . . who knows? The Kalahari is filled with big predators." It's not a comforting thought.

The sun is getting low in the sky. You're going to need to settle in. You feel like you should stay close to the route of the tour bus. That's where they'll come looking for you. On the other hand, if this kill is fresh, whatever predator is responsible might be coming back. Or others might sniff it out. Do you really want to be nearby if it does?

- To leave this area, turn to page 54.
- To camp here, along the road, turn to page 56.

"Something big took down that springbok, and I'm betting it's going to come back for it," you tell Maria. "We need to put some distance between us and whatever that might be."

Maria nods. "Look over there," she says, pointing south. There's a rocky area over there. It might be a good place to wait out the night."

You shrug in agreement. The rocks might provide some protection. The two of you trek across the desert, reaching the rocky area just an hour or two before sunset. As you take a drink from your water canteen, you hear a strange hissing sound behind you. You turn to see a large, brown snake with dark bands on its back. It's curled into an S-shaped pattern with its head raised—and it's just a few feet away from Maria.

"Puff adder," you whisper. It's one of the deadliest and most aggressive snakes in the world. And it looks about to strike. You have to act fast.

- To grab Maria and pull her away from the snake, turn to page 61.
- To throw your canteen at the snake to scare it away, turn to page 67.

You scratch your head. "Look, there's nowhere we can go out here where we'll be completely safe from predators. So let's stay nearby. If rescue comes, we don't want to miss it."

There's a large acacia tree not far from where the bus was parked. "Let's climb up in there," you suggest. "It should keep us safe from most predators."

"Most?" Maria asks.

You shrug. "Well, leopards are climbers. I'm not sure if a lion would climb a tree, though. And wild dogs definitely won't."

So as the sun starts to dip below the horizon, the two of you hoist yourselves up onto a long branch that sticks out above the ground, out of the reach of any predators on the ground.

Soon, darkness falls over the desert. It's very still and mostly quiet. The heat of the day quickly fades, and a chill sets in.

You can't sleep up here, but you manage to relax a little while you wait. Then suddenly, a noise gets your heart pumping. It's a low growling sound. You scan the ground below. By the light of the moon, you make out an unmistakable form not far away. It's a lion. No . . . it's two lions. Three! The big cats must be out searching for prey. Have they smelled you already?

As you watch the three lions slowly move in your direction, you know the answer to that question. They know you're here. You and Maria make eye contact and somehow seem to agree to stay silent.

• Turn the page.

That's when you see the headlights. You hear the sound of a vehicle coming down the road. Someone is sweeping a bright spotlight across the ground. They're looking for you!

The jeep is moving at a fairly fast pace. They're never going to see you up in the tree. You try shouting, but you're far enough away that they probably don't hear you over the noise of the engine. What can you do?

- To stay in the tree and keep shouting, go to the next page.
- To scramble down and run to the jeep, turn to page 65.

58

You cry out, but no one hears you. You and Maria watch helplessly as the jeep passes by and disappears into the distance. You were too far away to flag it down, and you weren't going to risk chasing after it with lions on the prowl. It was your big chance to get out of here quickly, and now it's gone.

It's a long night. The lions ignore you, eventually moving on in search of other prey. By sunrise, you're cold, stiff, and ready to get your feet back on the ground.

You stand there for a moment, looking in all directions. To the south, behind a ridge, you see what looks like a cloud of dust.

"What's that?" you ask, pointing it out to Maria.

• Turn the page.

She just shakes her head. "Could be anything. It might be better to just head back to the road. We don't want to miss anyone else who comes along."

She's probably right. But your curiosity is killing you. "What if it's a search party? You can head back toward the road and I can go scout it out. Then we don't risk missing rescue if it comes. I'll come right back, whatever I find."

Maria scowls. "I don't know. Splitting up doesn't seem like a great idea. But it's up to you."

She has a point. Separating could be dangerous.

- To head back to the road with Maria, turn to page 63.
- To head toward the ridge to investigate, turn to page 74.

The puff adder looks ready to strike. With one swift motion, you grab Maria, jerking her away from the snake just before it lunges. You both crash to the ground. Luckily, the snake decides enough is enough and darts off in the opposite direction. It leaves a trail in the sand as it slithers away.

"Phew," Maria sighs. "That was close. Thanks."

"Don't say I never did anything for you," you tease, with a grin.

As you watch the sun set over the Kalahari, you reflect on your situation and how you're going to get through it. You were careless to wander away from the group. If someone doesn't find you soon, you and Maria could be in for serious trouble.

• Turn the page.

After a long, mostly sleepless night, the eastern sky begins to brighten. The sun is coming up. You should probably head back to the road. Help could arrive at any moment, and you don't want to miss it.

Go to the next page.

Maria leads the way as you trek back to the area where the tour bus left you. The sun gains strength by the hour, so you carefully ration what water remains in your canteens. Despite the heat, you find that you're not sweating very much. Your body must be dangerously low on water. The situation is getting critical. You don't know if you can survive another night out here.

"Look at that," Maria gasps, breaking you out of your thoughts. Not far away, along a line of rough brush, is a small animal. As you look closer, you realize that you're seeing something really special—a very young desert black rhino, not much bigger than a large dog. The little creature seems to be struggling. A section of some sort of mesh netting is wrapped around one of its hind legs. "Even way out here, these animals have to deal with our trash," you say with disgust.

• Turn the page.

The netting is wrapped in a way that causes the little rhino to stumble along. It can't extend its leg. You know that if nothing is done, even such a small thing could spell doom for the creature. But is there anything you can do? And what if its mother is nearby? Helping a manageable-sized wild baby animal is one thing. Facing down its full-grown mother is another.

• To try to help the little rhino, turn to page 69.
• To keep your distance, turn to page 71.

This could be your only chance. If the jeep drives by, who knows if it will come back? "We have to move!" you whisper urgently to Maria. As quietly as you can, you scramble down the trunk. As soon as your feet hit solid ground, you take off in a sprint to intercept the jeep.

Maria, who has always been a better athlete, quickly pulls ahead of you. You follow her in a mad dash, screaming at the top of your lungs all the way. The jeep stops. The spotlight swings in your direction, momentarily blinding you. But you don't mind because it means that they see you! You're going to make it!

• Turn the page.

Just as Maria hops into the jeep, something big, fast, and heavy slams into you from behind. Like all cats, lions are born to chase. As soon as they saw you two jump out of the tree, they gave chase. The lion drags you to the ground. Desperate, you try to break free. But it's no hope. You're doomed. Your last thought is of Maria. You won't make it, but you hope she will.

THE END

To follow another path, turn to page 9.
To learn more about life in the desert, turn to page 99.

You have to act fast, so you do the first thing that comes to mind. You hurl your canteen at the snake, hoping to scare it away.

It doesn't work. Your throw misses the puff adder by a few inches. With blinding speed, the snake strikes, sinking its long, sharp fangs into Maria's leg. She screams in pain and shock. The two of you quickly run away, scrambling up onto the rocks.

Maria is in a lot of pain. You know that the snake's venom will slowly work through her system. With medical attention, puff adder bites are rarely fatal. But you're a long way from medical help. And with the sun about to set, there's nothing you can do to help her. You just try to make her comfortable so that the two of you can make it to sunrise.

• Turn the page.

It's a night of misery. As the hours pass, Maria's condition grows worse. She vomits several times and can't even keep water down. The puff adder's venom is wreaking havoc on her body, and you know the clock is ticking. All you can do is distract her with childhood memories and silly jokes. Neither of you feel like laughing much, though.

By dawn, Maria is unconscious. Her breathing is shallow. You stay with her through the morning. She's sick, dehydrated, and the heat of the desert sun is quickly draining what little strength she has left. When a search team finds you late that afternoon, it's too late. You've lost your sister.

The guilt haunts you for the rest of your life. You can't help wishing the two of you had never wandered off. You should have known better.

THE END

To follow another path, turn to page 9.
To learn more about life in the desert, turn to page 99.

Your heart goes out to the little rhino. You've always had a soft spot for animals, and one of your childhood dreams was to become a veterinarian. You cannot resist the urge to help the struggling animal.

"Come on," you tell Maria. "Let's help the little guy."

You approach carefully. The rhino seems a bit nervous as you get closer, but with its leg bound, it can't run away.

"Easy little guy," you say in a calm voice. Gently, you touch the rhino's back. Its skin is warm and rough. Slowly, you begin to unwrap the netting. It takes a little tugging, but you finally pull it loose.

"Got it!" you say triumphantly. It feels so good to have been able to help.

• Turn the page.

"Umm . . . we have company," Maria says with a quiver in her voice.

You look up just in time to see another rhino charging at you. Its head is down and its horn is pointed directly at you. There's just enough time for you to realize that it must be the baby's mother. And she doesn't want you anywhere near her little one.

It all happens in a heartbeat. The rhino is huge, but shockingly fast. You try to scramble away, but it's too late. She's bearing down, and there's nothing you can do about it.

All you can do is hope Maria gets away. You're not going to survive this wildlife encounter.

THE END

To follow another path, turn to page 9.
To learn more about life in the desert, turn to page 99.

You desperately want to help the little rhino. But this is the wild Kalahari, not a petting zoo. If there's a young rhino here, its mother can't be far away.

You sigh, shake your head, and continue on. The temperature is soaring. Your water is going fast, and you've both been sweating heavily in the heat of the day. Your bodies won't last long once the water is gone. Do you need to start planning for another night out here?

Just as you begin to panic, everything changes. You spot a cloud of dust in the distance. You know immediately what it is.

• Turn the page.

A vehicle! You and Maria run toward it, waving your arms and shouting. The small 4x4 pickup truck pulls to a stop. A tall man in a park ranger uniform steps out and runs to you. "Thank goodness we finally found you," he says in a heavy accent. "Your parents have been so worried! We all have!"

You climb into the truck and sink into a seat as you head back to safety. It's been a wild adventure, and you're glad to see it come to an end.

THE END

To follow another path, turn to page 9.
To learn more about life in the desert, turn to page 99.

You could just wait around in hopes of being rescued. But you'd rather do everything in your power to help yourself. "I think I should check it out," you tell Maria. "It's not very windy. I don't know what could kick up dust like that, other than vehicles."

So you head off. The ridge is farther away than it looked. The hike is a bigger investment of energy—and water—than you thought it would be. But there's no turning back now.

When you finally reach the top of the ridge, you see a fantastic sight. It's a herd of wildebeests! They were once common in the Kalahari, but their numbers are much lower now. It's not what you'd hoped to find, but it's an amazing sight. The herd is so close—you can hear their grunts and smell their scent. There must be hundreds of them!

Suddenly, the wildebeests freeze. They've spotted something. A predator! So they do what comes naturally. They run.

For a moment, the idea of a predator scares you. Then, too late, you realize the real danger. It's a stampede. Hundreds of huge wildebeests charging straight at you!

You turn and run. But it's hopeless. The herd is too big. Too fast. They're not out to hurt you. They're just protecting themselves. But the end result is the same as if they were. Your adventure is over.

THE END

To follow another path, turn to page 9.
To learn more about life in the desert, turn to page 99.

CHAPTER 4

ADVENTURE DOWN UNDER

The snap of your camera's shutter clicks as you take a series of photographs of tall limestone pinnacles jutting out of a sea of sand.

"Pretty cool, huh?" you say to Daisy. She replies with a single bark.

You're a photojournalist on assignment in Australia, and you've taken your black Lab with you. Daisy bounds off through the sand, searching for wildlife to sniff out.

• Turn the page.

After spending the first part of your trip in highly populated areas of eastern Australia, you've now moved into the heart of the continent—the Outback. You're roughing it out here, sleeping under the stars in the bed of your rented pickup. And your journey has taken you into some of the most hostile—and beautiful—landscapes you've ever seen. Huge sand dunes roll like waves across the endless desert. Ancient rock formations dot the land. Small rivers and saltwater lakes cut through the rough terrain. They are gathering places for the animals that call this desolate place home.

As you click through some of the images on your camera, Daisy suddenly starts barking.

"Hush, Daisy!" you call out. But she just keeps barking. You set down your camera and go see what she's barking at.

"What is it, girl?" you ask. Daisy stands before one of the limestone pillars, where dry brush grows up out of the desert sand.

At first, you don't see anything. Then you notice a large spiderweb. It's a mess of random strands—not a neat, orderly spiderweb. And crawling out from under the web is a black spider with a bright red back. You've never seen anything quite like it. It looks beautiful and terrifying all at the same time.

Daisy barks again at the spider. You can tell that she is about to go after it.

- To let Daisy go after the spider, turn to page 80.
- To sweep the spider away with your hand, turn to page 82.

You chuckle at Daisy as she barks at the little spider. You think it might be a redback spider. You don't know a lot about them, except that Australians sometimes joke about them biting people on the toilet. If the locals think it's so funny, how dangerous could it really be?

Daisy finally collects her courage and snaps at the spider. But it's quick. In a flash, the spider whirls around and delivers a bite right to Daisy's snout. Your Lab yelps and bolts away. All you can do is laugh.

"Daisy, you asked for that one," you tell her, stroking her head. "Come on, let's see what else we can find."

It's a busy day, searching for scorpions, snakes, and more, and the bite is soon forgotten. But that night, Daisy doesn't seem like herself. Her snout is swollen. She seems tired. You're not too worried. "Nothing a good night of sleep won't cure," you tell her, laying down in your sleeping bag in the back of the truck. And with that, you drift off under a starry sky.

Turn to page 90.

"Daisy, no!" you say in a stern voice. You don't want your best poochie pal to get bit by a spider. You reach down and sweep the spider away with the back of your hand. You've heard redback spiders are venomous. But their bites really aren't that dangerous to healthy people. And you act quickly enough that the spider never even gets the chance to bite you. It tumbles onto the sand below and quickly scurries under the rock.

You and Daisy continue your journey through the Outback. It's breathtaking. You feel like you're the only person in the world out here. Along the way, you come to a small river winding through the land. You follow it to a large saltwater lake.

It seems strange to see a body of water in the middle of the desert. But rains to the south have filled rivers that flow inland. Life springs up around the lake.

You walk down to the shore, where you notice a strange shape near the edge of the water. You could swear you saw a pair of eyes above the surface, but when you do a double take, there's nothing there.

Your curiosity is piqued. Part of you wants to get a closer look. But it might be safer to start snapping photos from here.

- To take photos from here, turn to page 84.
- To go to the shoreline for a better look, turn to page 92.

Daisy starts to growl at the water, so you decide that getting closer might not be a great idea. It's a wise choice. A few minutes later, the shape resurfaces. This time, there's no doubt in your mind what you are seeing. It's a very large saltwater crocodile! You're glad you're a safe distance away. But you're also close enough to get some really good shots. You quickly fire off a series of photos. Soon, the big reptile disappears again.

"Wow, Daisy!" you say with delight. "These are going to be some of our best shots!"

It's not the only big reptile you see that day. Later, as you and Daisy hike along some rough, rocky terrain, you spot a large monitor lizard. As you take some photos, Daisy creeps up for a closer look. She sniffs at the big lizard from a car's length away. She seems nervous, so you don't think she'll get any closer. This would be a really cool photo. But is Daisy safe? Maybe you should call her back. But doing that might spook the lizard too.

- To call Daisy back, turn to page 86.
- To get a cool photo of Daisy with the lizard, turn to page 88.

"Daisy!" you call sharply. "Come!"

The black Lab hesitates for a moment. She's fascinated by the big lizard, and she really wants to play with this new friend. But you know a monitor lizard has a nasty bite. It's not worth the risk. As Daisy scampers back, the lizard crawls away.

You spend the next three days roaming the Australian Outback. You get some really cool shots of a tiny thorny devil lizard and a brown scorpion. Then, on your last day, you come across something really interesting—a pack of dingoes. You spot them from the distance, and you know you need some good photos. Dingoes are one of Australia's most famous animals. The wild dogs are apex predators out here—meaning that they're at the top of the food chain.

Even from a distance, Daisy can smell the dingoes. She's eager to check out this strange scent. You're going to go for a closer look, but you're not sure you trust her to go with you—even on her leash. On the other hand, a pack of dingoes could be dangerous. Daisy might make them think twice about attacking you.

- To take Daisy with you to check out the dingoes, turn to page 94.
- To leave Daisy behind and head out alone, turn to page 96.

What a cool photo opportunity! You kneel down, lift up your camera, and snap a few shots. The big lizard stays perfectly still as Daisy inches closer and closer, sniffing away. Then suddenly, it whirls around and snaps at her. The monitor lizard bites her on her leg. Daisy yelps in pain as she runs to you. You should have never been so careless!

You use your canteen to wash out the bite marks on Daisy's leg. Then you wrap it in an old T-shirt you have in the truck.

"It's been a long day, let's get some sleep," you tell her as you lay your sleeping bag out in the back of the truck. She curls up next to you. But she sleeps restlessly. In the middle of the night, she's up whimpering. Is the bite infected?

You hope not. But there's nothing you can do about it now. If she's not doing better in the morning, you'll take her to a vet. You gently pet her until she calms down again, then the two of you drift back off to sleep.

Turn the page.

By the morning, Daisy isn't doing well. You climb out of the truck and stretch. But when you call her, Daisy barely lifts her head to look at you. She's panting a lot, and her eyes have a glassy sort of stare.

You sit down next to her and stroke her black fur. She feels warm to the touch. "Not feeling so well, huh girl?" you say in a soothing voice. There was so much you still wanted to see and do on your photo safari. You had hoped to take pictures of snakes, scorpions, and more rock formations. But now those hopes are dashed.

"We'd better get you to a veterinarian," you tell Daisy. It'll be hours of driving before you get to a town big enough to have a vet. With only a little bit of time left in your trip Down Under, you know you probably won't make it back out here again.

But Daisy's your best friend, and nothing is more important than her. So you start up the truck and say farewell to the wild Outback.

THE END

To follow another path, turn to page 9.
To learn more about life in the desert, turn to page 99.

"Interesting," you mutter to yourself as you move closer to the shoreline. You peer out over the water. A series of ripples trace a line on the water's surface, but you can't make out any shapes underneath.

You kick off your shoes and wade into the water. It's very warm. You're about knee-deep when Daisy suddenly starts to growl. You turn to tell her to quiet down, when suddenly there's a loud splashing right in front of you. A large shape lunges out of the water—directly at you.

Startled, you try to back up. But you stumble, falling over backward into the water.

That's bad news. Because now it's clear exactly what's coming at you—a large saltwater crocodile. The big reptile opens its jaws and snaps them shut onto your leg.

You scream, desperately trying to escape its clutches. But it's too late. The croc is too strong. It's dragging you down, and you're helpless to escape. Your adventure is about to end in disaster. You just hope Daisy will be okay.

THE END

To follow another path, turn to page 9.
To learn more about life in the desert, turn to page 99.

"All right, you can come," you tell Daisy. She whines when you put the leash on her. You haven't used it in weeks. "Sorry," you tell her. "Gotta have it for this adventure."

Together, you strike off into the desert. Daisy pulls on her leash, eager to get closer to the wild dogs. She can smell the dingoes from a long way away. Unfortunately, they can smell her too. Just as you start to get close enough to see the dingoes clearly, they raise their heads. They've spotted you.

Your heart races, but you don't have anything to fear. The dingoes want nothing to do with you. Together, they prance off into the distance. You never even had a chance to get the photos you wanted.

You sigh. Your journey through the Australian Outback is coming to an end. It's time to go home. You just wish you'd gotten those last photos. It was a great trip regardless, but photos of a wild dingo pack would have made it just about perfect.

THE END

To follow another path, turn to page 9.
To learn more about life in the desert, turn to page 99.

"Sorry girl," you tell Daisy. "I won't be long."

You turn up the air conditioning and leave Daisy behind. You're always careful when you leave her in the truck. The heat of the sun can be dangerous inside a vehicle. But you'll only be a few minutes. Daisy whines a bit at being left behind. But you know that bringing her could only complicate matters.

You creep closer to the pack. They are aware of you. But as long as you don't get too close, they don't seem to mind. They're apex predators, which means that they don't easily feel threatened. They're watchful but not afraid.

You kneel down, put a zoom lens on your camera, and start snapping shots. It's amazing. You get pictures of the whole pack—even a group of adorable pups wrestling. You've taken thousands of photos on your journey, but these are by far your favorites.

It's the perfect way to end the trip of a lifetime. It's time to head back to civilization—back home. But you've experienced the Outback in a way that few people ever have, and it's a memory that you'll never forget.

THE END

To follow another path, turn to page 9.
To learn more about life in the desert, turn to page 99.

CHAPTER 5

LIFE IN THE DESERT

Deserts cover more than 20 percent of Earth's land. And they all have one thing in common. They're dry, averaging less than 10 inches (25 centimeters) of precipitation each year. Many people think of deserts as hot—and a lot of them are. But they don't have to be. Every continent on Earth has deserts—even frigid Antarctica.

The dry conditions of deserts make life challenging for the plants and animals that live in them. All life on Earth depends on water. In deserts, where that precious resource is hard to come by, survival is a constant battle. Each desert species has adapted to survive, and even thrive, in these harsh landscapes.

Many desert plants, such as cactuses, have adapted to collect water during rare wet periods. They have shallow, widespread root systems that quickly collect rainwater. They store this water deep inside the body of the plant. Thick, waxy skin prevents it from evaporating. Many plants are covered with sharp spikes. The spikes deter animals from getting at the water stored inside. During especially dry times, many plants go dormant. They may look dead. But they're just waiting for the water to return to spring back to life.

Plants aren't alone in their efforts to store water. Many desert animals do the same thing. Camels can drink gallons of water at a time and store most of it for dry times ahead. Camels also store large deposits of fat in their humps. This lets them go without food for months at a time. Life in the desert is all about making scarce resources last as long as possible.

In very hot deserts, some animals adapt by being nocturnal. Temperatures can soar during the daylight hours—even reaching 130 degrees Fahrenheit (54 degrees Celsius) or higher! So animals such as foxes spend this time tucked away in dens, where it's much cooler. They come out to search for food at night when temperatures drop.

Many animals adapt by getting all the water they need from their food. Turkey vultures don't need to drink water at all. Another desert animal called the kangaroo rat never drinks! They're so specialized to desert life that even in captivity, they won't drink water even when it's given to them!

Competition for resources in the desert is fierce. Animals are in a constant battle for survival. For many of these creatures, such as spiders, scorpions, and snakes, venom and poison are important weapons. They use them as a defense. Most predators will think twice about trying to eat venomous or poisonous prey. Venomous and poisonous animals also use these weapons to kill their own prey.

Humans in the desert face all of the same challenges that plants and animals do. And the solutions that work for wildlife can work for people as well. Two of the biggest dangers to people are dehydration and heat exposure. The human body needs 11.5 to 16 cups (2.7 to 3.7 liters) of water per day, although people can get by with less in the short term. That's more than most people can carry with them. One way to conserve water is to not sweat. That means finding shade and resting during the hottest times of the day.

Luckily, survival experts consider food a low priority in short-term situations. Some suggest not eating at all. The body uses water to digest food. It may be better to conserve that water by not eating.

Of course, wildlife can also pose a major threat to humans—and not just a large predator. A bite or sting from a venomous creature can drain the body of precious resources. Larger predators may then see a weakened human as an easy meal. Building a fire at night can help keep many animals at bay.

Deserts are one of the harshest climates on Earth. Resources are scarce. Help may be a long way away. By keeping calm and making good decisions, people can give themselves an edge. It might just be enough to help them survive a dangerous situation.

Mauro Prosperi

In 1994, Mauro Prosperi of Italy got lost when competing in a race in the Sahara. Prosperi did what he could to survive. He ate bats, insects, and reptiles. He drank his own urine. After nine days in the scorching desert, Prosperi finally found a village and was rescued. His ordeal took a heavy toll on his health. He lost 35 pounds (16 kilograms), but he eventually recovered.

Aron Ralston

Wildlife isn't the only danger in the desert. In 2003, Aron Ralston was out hiking in Utah's Bluejohn Canyon when his arm got pinned under a huge boulder. Ralston was trapped there for five days with little food or water. Ralston eventually used a pocketknife to cut off his own hand and part of his arm. He then hiked out of the canyon until he found people who could help him.

Albert Bojone

In 2011, South African park ranger Albert Bojone was in search of a group, or pride, of Kalahari lions. They had crossed out of the border of the Kgalagadi Transfrontier Park. He and a few others were hoping to move the lions back into the park. But when they found the pride, everything went wrong. One lion attacked. It jumped onto Bojone's truck and bit him. Bojone scrambled to the roof of the vehicle. A fellow park ranger had to shoot the lion to rescue Bojone, who eventually recovered from his injuries.

John Waddell

In 2018, John Waddell lowered himself into an abandoned gold mine in the desert of Arizona. The treasure hunt quickly went wrong, though. Waddell's climbing equipment broke, leaving him stranded. To make matters worse, the mine was filled with deadly rattlesnakes. For two days, Waddell fought for his life. He had to kill three of the snakes to avoid being bitten. Rescue finally came, and Waddell amazingly survived his ordeal.

This book looks at what it might be like to survive wildlife encounters in the desert. Here are some more ideas to think about.

Throughout history, people have called deserts home. In modern times, many live in cities and towns in the desert. But that hasn't always been the case. What might it have been like to live in the desert in prehistoric times? How would you have adapted and survived? Would you have had what it took to call such a harsh environment home?

Often, people lost in the desert need rescue. But that's a lot of work for the people who need to go out and search for them. If you were one of the rescuers, how would you feel? What clues would you look for? And how would you help people when you found them?

Deserts aren't the only place where people encounter dangerous wildlife. What other sorts of environments might lead to life-or-death encounters? What sorts of animals might you face? And which encounters would scare you the most?

GLOSSARY

arid (AR-id)—dry

dehydration (dee-hy-DRAY-shuhn)—a life-threatening medical condition caused by a lack of water

dormant (DOR-muhnt)—in an inactive state

nocturnal (nok-TUR-nuhl)—active at night and resting during the day

photo safari (FO-to suh-FAH-ree)—a trip in which a person takes photographs of wild animals

precipitation (pri-sip-i-TAY-shuhn)—water that falls from the clouds in the form of rain, hail, or snow

predator (PRED-uh-tur)—an animal that hunts other animals for food

prey (PRAY)—an animal hunted by other animals as food

ration (RASH-uhn)—to limit to prevent running out of something

symptom (SIMP-tuhm)—something that shows someone has an illness

venom (VEN-uhm)—a poisonous liquid produced by some animals

BIBLIOGRAPHY

Alloway, David. *Desert Survival Skills.* Austin, TX: University of Texas Press, 2000.

Cartanio, Carol. *Myths & Truths about Coyotes.* Birmingham, AL: Menasha Ridge Press, 2011.

Cooper, Bob. *Outback Survival.* Sydney: Hachette Australia, 2012.

Davies, Barry. *SAS Desert Survival.* New York: Simon & Schuster, 2012.

Snakebites: First Aid mayoclinic.org/first-aid/first-aid-snake-bites/basics/art-20056681

Urbigkit, Cat. *When Man Becomes Prey: Fatal Encounters with North America's Most Feared Predators.* Guilford, CT: Lyons Press, 2014.

READ MORE

Doeden, Matt. *Can You Survive Hair-Raising Mountain Encounters?: An Interactive Wilderness Adventure.* North Mankato, MN: Capstone, 2023.

Eason, Sarah. *Desert Survival Guide.* New York: Crabtree, 2021.

Jaycox, Jaclyn. *This or That Questions About the Desert.* North Mankato, MN: Capstone, 2022.

INTERNET SITES

Desert Biomes
ducksters.com/science/ecosystems/desert_biome.php

Desert Habitat
kids.nationalgeographic.com/nature/habitats/article/desert

Desert Survival Skills
desertusa.com/desert-activity/desert-survival-skills.html

Matt Doeden is a freelance author and editor from Minnesota. He's written numerous children's books on sports, music, current events, the military, extreme survival, and much more. His books *Sandy Koufax* (Twenty-First Century Books, 2006) and *Tom Brady: Unlikely Champion* (Twenty-First Century Books, 2011) were Junior Library Guild selections. Doeden began his career as a sportswriter before turning to publishing. He lives in Minnesota with his wife and two children.